Olivia Lauren's
OCCUPATIONS A TO Z
A Children's Guide To Jobs And Careers

Melissa-Sue John, Ph.D.
Youth Illustrators: Simonne-Anais and Zachary-Michael Clarke

© 2017 LAUREN SIMONE PUBLISHING HOUSE

All rights reserved. In accordance with the U.S. Copyright Act of 1976, the scanning, uploading, and electronic sharing of any part of this book without the permission of the publisher constitute unlawful piracy and theft of the author's intellectual property. If you would like to use material from the book (other than for review purposes), prior written permission must be obtained by contacting the publisher at laurensimonepubs@gmail.com.

Library of Congress Cataloging-in-Publication Data
John, Melissa-Sue.
Olivia Lauren's Occupations A to Z: A Children's Guide to Jobs and Careers/ Melissa-Sue John (Author), Simonne-Anais Clarke and Zachary-Michael Clarke (Illustrators)
p. cm.
ISBN-13: 978-0-9979520-2-5 (soft cover)
ISBN-10:0997952024
1. Occupation 2. Jobs 3. Careers 4. Actors 5. STEM I. John, Melissa-Sue II. Series
2017900153

To My daughters, Alyssa John and Olivia John,

for their inspiration.

Matthew John, Yolanda-Mitsy White-Aiken, and Clover Crumbie
for nudging me to write my stories.

Faith Clarke, Kareen Hartley, and Rose-Anne Uwague
who assisted in proofreading.

Aa

Accountants are book keepers. They keep record of money that people or companies receive and spend.

Actors, like me, play characters on stage, at theaters, in movies, or on television to entertain viewers like you!

Affirmative Action Officers work in human resources. They increase the different types of people and help them feel included.

Ambassadors are high-ranking persons who represent his or her government while living in another country.

Anesthesiologists are doctors trained to give patients pain medicine (known as anesthesia) before a medical procedure to lessen the pain.

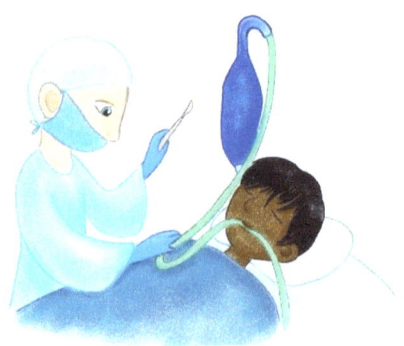

Animators use computers to create cartoons, anime, and other animated movies.

Anthropologists are trained to study different groups of people from tribes, cultures, urban communities, and societies.

Archeologists are trained to find clues about historical events by studying bones, fossils, and tools of ancient people and animals. Some archeologists discovered dinosaur bones.

Artists are creative people who draw, paint, write, design, create, or perform.

Astronauts travel in a spacecraft and explore outer space.

Astronomers study the stars, planets, and other things in outer space.

Attendants, such as assistants, care takers, flight attendants, customer representatives or ushers, take care of and serve others.

Athletes are well-trained people that compete in sports and events. My friend, below, loves track and field.

Auditors are special types of accountants who inspect a person's or company's records.

Authors write articles, reports, stories, or books.

Bb

Bakers make dough and batter and cook them in an oven using dry heat to create breads, cakes, and pastries.

Bank Tellers deposit or withdraw money for customers at a bank.

Barbers cut hair and shave beards.

Basketball Players play in competitive games involving two five-player teams. The team who scores the most points by throwing the basketball into their net wins.

Bee Keepers breed and take care of bees. Without bees, we would not have any food.

Bloggers write articles about their opinions, activities, and experiences and post to a website.

Botanists study and care for plants. They teach us about the parts of a plant, species type, and the environment.

Cc

Chefs are professional cooks in charge of a kitchen in a restaurant, hotel, or on a cruise ship.

Chemists conduct research and carry out chemical experiments.

Choreographers arrange dance steps for dancers.

Civil Engineers design bridges, roads, dams, and large buildings.

Computer Engineers develop and test computer software.

Computer Programmers arrange signals, letters, or numbers for a computer program to function properly.

Dd

Dentists treats diseases and conditions that affect gums and teeth.

Dermatologists treat diseases and conditions that affect the skin.

Designers create, plan, invent, draw, or make something new.

Disc Jockeys play popular music on the radio or at a club or event.

Doctors (also known as **Physicians**) are trained to keep people healthy or help them recover from illness or injury.

Dog Trainers are persons who train and coach dogs, usually to work with police.

Dog Walkers help dogs to get their needed daily exercise.

Ee

Electrical Engineers work with electricity.

Electricians install and maintain electrical equipment.

Entertainers, like Actors, **Comedians, Clowns, Musicians,** or **Singers,** perform for an audience.

Entrepreneurs organize, run, and promote their own business.

Epidemiologists study how diseases are spread and how to stop them from getting worse.

Ff

Farmers improve the soil to grow food and raise farm animals such as chickens, goats, pigs, or cows.

Fashion Designers create original clothing, accessories, and footwear.

Film Critics publish reviews of films.

Firefighters rescue people and animals from fires.

Fishers catch fish using nets, fishing rods, and traps for people to eat or put in their aquarium tanks.

Gg

Geographers study the earth, life on earth, and the effects of life on earth. They can tell us about different clouds or rocks.

Geologists study the solid and liquid that makes up the Earth. They tell us about earthquakes and floods.

Graphic Designers combine words and pictures for advertisements, magazines, or books.

Gymnasts display flexibility and skill on bars, beams, and in floor routines.

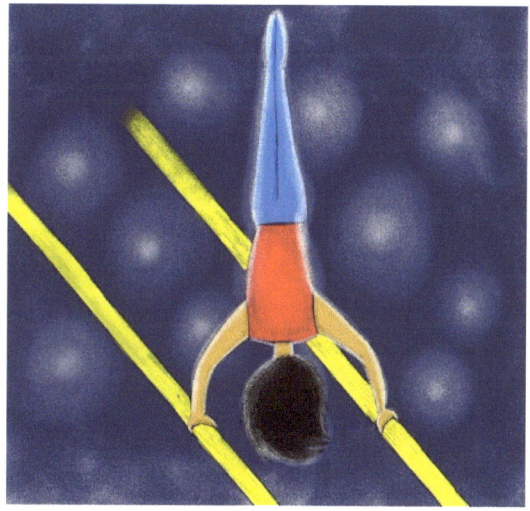

Hh

Hair Stylists wash, treat, cut, and style hair.

Historians are experts in the history of a period, region, or social problem.

Home Inspectors check houses for safety before a buyer buys it from the seller.

Hosts receive guests at a restaurant, an event, or to entertain people on a television show or radio program.

Human Resource Officers recruit, train, monitor, and counsel employees about their medical, dental, and retirement benefits.

Ii

Image Consultants review a person's wardrobe, attitude, and behavior, and give advice to help gain a job, promotion, romantic partner, or increase self-esteem.

Interior Decorators create and design homes and offices to the client's satisfaction.

Insurance Agents sell insurance policies and respond to accident reports.

Investigators, such as detectives, criminal investigators, journalistic investigators, search for information to explain the cause or wrongdoer of a problem.

Jj

Jailers, Guards, or **Wardens** are persons in charge of prisoners.

Janitors, such as **cleaners**, **caretakers**, and **custodians**, clean and care for a building.

Judges, or **Magistrates**, are appointed to decide on legal cases in court.

Journalists write for newspapers or magazines or tell the news for a radio station or television network.

Justice of the Peace performs marriage ceremonies and grant licenses.

Kk

Key Cutters copy and cut keys for locks.

A **King** is a man born into royalty to rule over a sovereign nation.

Kitchen Clerks check the amount and value of food products issued to kitchen from storeroom.

Kitchen Supervisors are responsible for the supervision of daily kitchen operations, such as cleaning the equipment, checking supplies, and rotating food stock.

Ll

Landscape Designers draw the layout of the land and choose where flowers, shrubs, and trees go to improve the beauty of the location.

Lawyers (also known as **Attorneys**) help people or companies in legal matters.

Librarians get, organize, manage, and distribute resources. They help us to find information and check out books from the library.

Life Guards, often seen at the pool or beach, try to prevent emergencies, and react to them by providing treatment until medical services arrive.

Mm

Marine Biologists study sea life and their habitat.

Marine Pilots help ships navigate through dangerous waters.

Mechanics fix power-driven things such as cars or trains.

Meteorologists predict the weather, so we can know what things we need to wear and whether we need an umbrella.

Models promote clothing, shoes, makeup, or other products for entertainment, marketing, and sales.

Movie Directors manage the camera crew and production staff.

Nn

Nail Technicians give manicures and pedicures to customers.

A **Nanny** is a full-time caregiver for children.

A **Notary** is authorized to certify documents.

Nurses are trained to help doctors and care for patients.

Nutritionists are trained to help people eat the right foods in the correct amount.

Nature Guides give tours through the forests.

Oo

Occupational Therapists help patients recover from physical injury or illness in order to perform regular activities such as walking.

Ophthalmologists specialize in medical and surgical care of the eyes and in prevention of eye disease or injury.

Opticians make and sell eye glasses and contact lens for the vision correction.

Optometrists examine eyes for visual defects and prescribe corrective lenses.

Orthodontists specialize and treat irregular placement of teeth and jaws, often using braces.

Orthopedic Doctors treats irregular alignment of bones and joints to prevent injury, pain, and harmful diseases.

Pp

Painters paint pictures, portraits, or walls.

Paramedics give first aid as a part of a police, rescue, or firefighting teams.

Pastors or **Priests** preach in churches or temples.

Personal Trainers help people reach their fitness goals.

Pharmacists make medicine for customers at a pharmacy.

Photographers take photos of nature or events.

Pilots or **Aviators** fly private or commercial planes.

Police Officers protect the innocent and enforce laws.

Politicians are elected officials such as a **Mayor** or **Senator**.

Postal Workers deliver mail and works for the postal service.

A **President** is a person elected to lead a country.

A **Principal** is the head of a school.

Psychologists study the mind and how it affects behavior.

Psychiatrists diagnose and treat mental illness.

Qq

Quality Control Specialists are responsible for making sure the products made meet the standards.

Quartermasters are military officers responsible for providing housing, food, clothing, and other supplies.

A **Queen** is a woman born into a royal family who leads a sovereign nation.

Quick Sketch Artist draws a portrait based on descriptions provided by a witness to help solve crimes.

Rr

Rabbis are Jewish leaders that work in a synagogue.

Real Estate Agent or **Realtor** shows land or houses to buyers on behalf of the seller.

Registrars help students register for college.

Reporters tell the news or conducts interviews for a broadcast.

Restaurant Owners manages a restaurant or food chain.

Ss

Sales Associates help customers with their purchases.

Scientists use observation and experimentation to gain knowledge in social, physical, or natural sciences.

Security Guards protect buildings from intruders.

Software Engineers develop, test, and make sure computer software work.

Song Writers create lyrics for songs and new music.

A **Sound Engineer** is a technician who works with audio for a broadcast, musical performance, or voice over.

Tt

Tailors make custom fit clothing for customers.

Talent Agent finds jobs for actors, singers, or other performers.

Tax Advisors are certificated accountants, attorneys, or financial advisors who help clients limit expenses while following the law.

Teachers (also known as **Instructors**, **Lecturers**, or **Professors**) pass on knowledge to students about a particular subject or train them in a certain skill set.

Translators interpret foreign languages to a person's native language.

Uu

Ushers show people to their seats at churches or event venues.

Upholsterers fix broken or damaged furniture.

Umpires or **Referees** watch competitive games or matches closely to make sure that the rules are being followed.

Vv

Vending Machine Attendant stocks vending machines with food or beverages.

Vendors sell goods and products to buyers and customers.

Veterinarians help maintain healthiness and treat diseased or hurt animals.

Violinists play the violin professionally for audiences.

Ww

Waiters take food and beverages from the kitchen to the customers in the dining area of a restaurant.

Web Designers create websites for individuals or companies for marketing purposes.

Web Developers specialize in the making of web applications to run from server to the web browser.

Writers compose essays, novels, stories, plays, articles, or reports.

Xx

X-ray Inspectors check that the x-ray machine is functioning.

X-Ray Technicians take and review x-rays of patients.

Yy

Yard Supervisors oversee the staff responsible for keeping the grounds of a train yard safe.

Yard Workers maintain the yard of a house or company.

Zz

Zoo Keepers are staff members responsible for feeding and maintaining animals at a zoo.

A **Zoo Veterinarian** maintains the health and wellness of zoo animals, and treat them when sick or injured.

A **Zoologist** studies the behavior, classification, and structure of animals.

www.ingramcontent.com/pod-product-compliance
Lightning Source LLC
Chambersburg PA
CBHW040020050426
42452CB00002B/68